MW01028623

50

Ways You Can Improve Your Memory

Dennis P. Swiercinsky, Ph.D.

World Wisdom, Inc.
Mission, Kansas

ISBN 0-9641311-0-2

Printed in the United States of America

10 9 8 7 6 5 4 3 2   95 96 97 98 99

The contents of this publication are not intended to render medical advice. While the ideas presented may provide a foundation for memory improvement, they must never be considered a substitute for direct advice concerning memory problems that may be a result of physical illness or injury. In such cases, direct consultation with a physician, psychiatrist, psychologist, or other appropriate health professional is necessary.

World Wisdom, Inc.
P. O. Box 1611
Mission, KS 66222
Telephone: (913) 262-4182
Facsimile: (913) 262-8174

Contents

Acknowledgments

Grateful acknowledgment is made to two individuals who helped immeasurably in completing this book. Sheila Vadovicky, my loyal and trusted colleague in psychological practice for seven years, read the initial draft of the book and provided critical comments and suggestions. Jane Guthrie, who has edited my writings for 10 years, provided many suggestions and the polish that makes the final work readable.

Preface

Many memory training books are full of instruction and exercises for remembering long numbers, random lists of words, and other useless information. Typically these books teach you how to develop bizarre visual associations or use cumbersome word association patterns in order to remember things. A person could spend a lot of time learning such techniques, only to find them often useless for everyday, practical applications. What you may have after all that concerted effort is the ability to impress party guests by quickly memorizing long lists of items, stock quotes, names and faces, and the like.

For immediately improving and gaining confidence in everyday memory, this book provides 50 simple, straightforward, no-gimmick tips and techniques that you can implement right away without much effort. The principles described here require no elaborate learning or extensive practice. Each tip, in its own right, taken alone, can help your memory immediately. These tips and techniques will gradually become part of how you think and do things, giving you confidence in your ability to learn new information and recall it easily, to minimize absentminded forgetfulness, to remember things more reliably, and simply to feel more comfortable with your day-to-day mental functioning.

Memory improvement depends on two essential ingredients: attitude and some basic skills. First, you must truly believe that you have an efficient memory potential and that you wish merely to improve on it. (If you cling to the image of a faulty memory, this "leaky boat" self-concept will set you up for permanent failure.) Second, you must continually add new mental skills that improve memory. The techniques and principles you will learn in this book focus on developing both the proper *attitude* for a good memory and the proper *techniques* for permanently improving your day-to-day functional learning and memory.

This book applies to anyone—high school and college students, business professionals, homemakers, retired persons—who has a reasonably healthy brain. In fact, most of the ideas have been used very successfully with persons who have sustained brain damage because of trauma, stroke, or illness.

Each of the learning and memory improvement pointers comes from many years of professional application; hence, each is "tried and true" based on sound psychological principles and successful results. Of course, just reading this book is not sufficient to improve your memory; you must commit yourself to practicing the thoughts that reinforce the attitudes and practicing the techniques so they become second nature to you.

Learning cannot be separated from memory. If we don't learn something in the first place, how can we remember it? Too often people think they have forgotten something when they really never learned—and remembered—it in the first place. You will notice that many of the pointers pertain to improving learning of new information as opposed only to recall of old information. A focus on *both* learning and memory must go hand in hand.

The best way to go about using this book is to skim it first all the way through. (The principles appear more or less in the order in which they should be learned, focusing first mainly on attitude building and later mainly on skill building.) Then, take each tip in turn and practice using it for a day or two. Add a new pointer every day or every other day. In no time at all you will have experienced the fundamental means by which your everyday memory can become as efficient as you wish to make it, within the natural capacity of your brain. By the time you reach tip number 50, you will have realized that the whole concept of a great memory is more than just the sum of these individual tips. A well-functioning memory goes hand in hand with a person who sincerely believes in his or her mental capacities and who knows how to take control of them. Therefore, resist feeling frustrated if you don't "succeed" as fast as you think you should. Patience and faithful practice will pay off.

50

Ways You Can Improve Your Memory

1

Repeat What You Want to Remember

When someone tells you something, repeat it back right away. By immediately saying back information told to you, you rehearse it in your own words. You've also experienced the act of recalling, right away, exactly what you want to remember later. Repeating back gives the person telling you something the opportunity to make sure you've got it right, too.

If you want to remember something you hear on a television or radio program or while listening to a tape, and you don't have the opportunity to write it down immediately, repeating the information to yourself out loud will help you remember it later. It is easier to remember things we say than things we hear.

A good way to learn a person's name is to use it, right away and often. When you're introduced to someone, repeat his or her name immediately: "Hello, Mr. Newman. Good to meet you. Nice-looking tie you're wearing." If the name is unusual, ask how it is spelled and then spell it back. Use the name again as soon as you can. Make a remark about it. Link the name to something noticeable about the person and you'll strengthen your memory even more.

Even repeating a person's name one time will enhance your remembering it many times over. Using the name a couple more times during conversation and again when saying good-bye will plant it in your memory even more solidly. You will have developed a mental image of a real person and not merely a meaningless memory of a name. You won't forget because you've really learned it. Remember, the key to good memory is good learning in the first place.

When learning new information or remembering something that someone tells you (such as an appointment date, a fact, or an idea), repeating it back energizes additional parts of your brain. Not only are the hearing parts of your brain energized when listening to someone, but the speech parts are energized, too. When you repeat back information, wider areas of memory circuits are put into action.

We are passive about much of what we hear. We hear in a physical sense, but we don't really hear in the mental sense that we comprehend what comes in through our ears. We can hear something but not "get it." Repeating information back as soon as you first hear it gets you involved. You demonstrate interest and involvement in the information you want to remember. The process thus becomes *active* instead of remaining passive. The new information comes from *your* brain and *your* mouth, too!

Making It Work for You

The next time someone tells you something, echo the information in a way that implies you've "got it." Use this technique to the extreme at first and gradually decide if it's something you need to continue doing. You'll become more tuned in, on the spot, to how well this or any other techniques for enhancing memory work for you.

2

Affirm Your Memory Every Day

Repeat a positive mental affirmation at least once every day. Say to yourself something like "I have a strong, active memory." Or maybe "My memory is good now, and getting even better as I practice self-confidence and good memory strategies." If you first don't believe in yourself, you can never succeed—at anything. You must start your memory improvement with positive thoughts about yourself.

You'll find it's absolutely futile to attempt any kind of memory enhancement program if you start out with a negative attitude about yourself or your memory. If you believe you have a bad memory in the first place, you will have difficulty turning that belief around. You will see every memory improvement technique you try as a potential failure. Good memory *techniques* will never correct a bad memory *attitude*. Believe that you have a decent memory and a good *potential* to start with, and you will increase your ability to learn and implement the other 49 tips in this book for *increasing* your memory.

Memory capacity and efficiency vary with the individual, and unfortunately we berate ourselves whenever we think our memory is not as good as someone else's. So, start with the memory ability you have right now (without comparison with anyone else), believe it is good, and trust that learning and using additional memory techniques and attitudes will make it even better. Assume you are reading this book to improve your good memory, not to correct a bad memory.

Do not affirm your memory only with future-oriented beliefs such as "I *will* develop a good memory." This implies your memory is poor right now. Again, you will never be successful if you start out negatively! Instead, say to yourself, "I am improving my good memory right now by learning efficient techniques and enhancement aids." Repeat this or a similar affirmation several times a day until the idea becomes a natural part of you.

We all experience a memory slip once in a while. That is entirely normal and does not indicate failure. A positive belief in yourself lets you accept where you are now and opens the doors for your future.

Making It Work for You

Make up an affirmation that you feel comfortable with. It should be positive and present (instead of future) oriented. A good way to begin an affirmation is "I am . . . ." Make the statement personal by including a reference to some specific area of memory you are improving: names, foreign language words, facts from textbooks or lectures, day-to-day things, and so forth. An effective affirmation might be "I am remembering people's names now better and better because I am paying attention, immediately repeating the name, and linking it to the qualities of a real, caring person."

3

Jog Your Memory With Visual Prompts

Use visual cues as memory joggers. When you want to remember to mow the lawn when you get home from work, park the lawnmower next to the car door as you leave in the morning so you won't miss the visual cue when you drive in after work. If you want to remember to call and make a doctor's appointment in the morning, put your pill bottle inside your cereal bowl. (And set the cereal bowl in the middle of the kitchen counter where you won't miss seeing it.) If you want to remember to stop by the dry cleaners when you drop your children off at school, put a wire hanger on the door knob leading into the garage. If you want to remember to pick up fresh flowers tomorrow, put the empty vase in an unusual but very conspicuous place—like the front seat of the car. If you want to remember to do the laundry tonight, set the hamper in the middle of the living room or in front of the TV set.

These are examples of visual cues that jog your memory. They are like the "string-around-the-finger" reminder. We attach the string when we think of something we need to remember to do, and later, when we see it, we remember what it was we wanted to remember. Of course, the string around the finger is metaphorical for doing anything obvious and unusual that will serve as a constant reminder to ask yourself, "What's that there for?"

If you think of something important you need to do the next day just as you're drifting off to sleep, toss an object from your nightstand out into the middle of the bedroom floor. When you wake up in the morning, you'll see the object there in a most unusual place and be quickly reminded of what it means. (This saves waking yourself up enough to find the light, paper, and pencil and sitting up to write it down. Save your sleep and set up a cue!)

This memory aid is useful as long as the reminder cue (string, object on the floor, lawnmower, cereal bowl, and so forth) is extremely unusual and is something you'll notice conspicuously. You'll amaze yourself at how effective this technique really is. Use it when writing things down and being organized in other ways isn't easy, or practical, or you're about to drift off to sleep. There is nothing wrong with being creative—or even eccentric—with this technique.

Too often people say, "Oh, I hope I don't forget that." Hope doesn't make for a great memory. Action does. The moment you catch yourself saying or thinking, "I hope I don't forget that," do something that will make you responsible for remembering. Give hope a rest; take the action that will *assure* your memory.

Making It Work for You

Think of something you want to remember to do tomorrow. Even if you're sure you won't forget it, just for practice come up with something that will jog your memory tomorrow—a visual cue that you won't miss. Maybe even pin a little note to your underclothing. A little eccentric? It *will* work! Perhaps you want to remember to say "happy birthday" to your boss tomorrow. You know you have some of those little cake candles in your kitchen cupboard. Get one and put it on your briefcase or somewhere you can't avoid seeing it in the morning. The visual prompt *and its uniqueness* will remind you of exactly what you want to remember.

4

Make Lists to Order and Organize Your Memory

A lmost anything you want to remember can be turned into a list. Lists force mental organization and the consolidation of information. Lists make your thoughts and plans concise and orderly—easier for the memory to store and retrieve. They also remove the burden of worry about whether you'll remember.

You can make lists of everything from the ordered steps involved in solving quadratic equations to grocery shopping items, things to do today, people to buy holiday gifts for, things you can do to improve your memory, business contacts to make this week, and errands to accomplish tomorrow.

Lists force you to extract essential information or plans and order them in some way, such as by categories, priorities, or sequence. Lists also serve a purpose similar to writing things in a diary or journal: The act of writing causes you to remember information more strongly. (If you make a grocery list, then discover at the store that you left it at home, just having made it will likely enable you to purchase exactly what you had on the list.)

Any information that lends itself to being put in a *numbered* list should be organized as such. If you have 10 things on a list, it will be easier to remember them if you assign each one a number.

Once compiled, your lists for upcoming tasks, events, and so forth can be attached to the pages of a calendar or journal. List-making should not become obsessional, though, or you'll have them all over the house. As with any memory aid, use a technique if it works for the situation and don't overdo it.

Making It Work for You

Take a sheet of paper and number each line on the left. Now, think of all the things you *need* to accomplish today and write each one beside a number. Make another list for all the things you *want* to remember to accomplish but won't necessarily need to do today. A list should reflect a category of things (things to do, things to buy, calls to make), including priorities.

5
Lighten Up and Look for the Humor

Things we remember the easiest are often the most absurd, most exaggerated, most bizarre, or funniest. Unique information is learned and remembered much more easily than stuff that is hum-drum. Information stands out when it's different or associated with something farfetched or humorous.

Compose an appealing phrase or sentence to remember something on the spot. By doing this, you will have energized your brain's creativity in forming unusual visual and emotional links to whatever it is you want to remember. For example, if your spouse asks you to pick up the dry cleaning on the way from work, make up a silly sentence such as, "There's nothing dry about that cute clerk at the cleaner's. Sure, honey, be glad to." (Sometimes the sentence is better said silently to yourself!)

Associating a comical, or even ridiculous, visualized scene around something you want to remember further enhances your memory. It will enliven your motivation, too. If you need to pick up a loaf of bread on your way home from Spanish class, think of the Pillsbury Doughboy giggling, then push your finger into your soft belly and giggle (just like the television ads). If you're afraid a technique like this will get you locked in a rubber room, go ahead, take a chance! At least you won't forget what got you there.

We are often accused of taking things too seriously. When we become too serious we get tense and stressed. Then we become narrow minded, begin to make mistakes, and forget things. By finding as much humor and lightness in things as possible, we relax, enjoy ourselves more, and remember things more easily.

Making It Work for You

Think of something or someone about which you want to have a strong memory. Get a mental picture of that person or thing. Name it; put it in a context; associate it with something else. Now, think of or make up something funny, ridiculous, or bizarre about it. Develop the thought strongly enough to make you smile, or better yet, laugh. Think you'll forget it now?

Learning to lighten up can benefit most people in numerous ways. Looking for humor, taking yourself less seriously, practicing laughter, easing up on self-demands—all these things remove stress from the mind. When the mind is less stressed it functions much more efficiently—especially in learning and remembering.

6

Learn Something New Every Day

New learning keeps your brain fresh and stimulated with new ideas, concepts, and challenges. A new idea or fact—even just a new word—helps build mental bridges that link information and makes it easier to retrieve. Regardless of your age or occupation, taking in a college course, workshop, seminar, magazine article, educational film, book, or lecture on some new topic keeps the brain energized for fresh information and makes learning and remembering fun. Reading, conversation, a visit to a museum, or an educational television program can provide readily available sources of information from which to learn something new every day.

This is not to suggest that new learning activities should be inordinately challenging. Do what you can without pushing yourself and making learning a drudgery. Just be aware that you are learning something every time you listen to a lecture, read a magazine article, or have a stimulating conversation. Instead of doing these things passively, enhance awareness of your active involvement in learning by taking notes, doodling, visualizing, or using some other memory aid. Learning is exciting. Being able to get excited about learning is the key to a great memory.

Every day, write down something you learned during that day. Keep a journal or note cards on which to record what you learn. Learning, and then remembering what you learn, is reinforcing; learning and remembering force thinking and the establishment of mental connections. Rich mental connections enhance later recall.

Learning something new every day keeps you focused on the fact that you *are* learning and remembering. At the same time, you'll begin to experience a mental richness in knowledge that will enhance your self-confidence. Remember, you cannot overload your memory if what you learn makes sense and is exciting and fun.

Making It Work for You

What new thing or idea did you learn today? Did you write it down in a journal or on a note card? If you can't think of something you've learned today, then where can you go or what can you do to seek some new tidbit of knowledge? Go do it!

A new word is a great place to start in learning something new every day. A large vocabulary does not overload the brain. In fact, knowing and learning lots of words provides just that much more to hang your thoughts (and memories) on. Use word-a-day calendars or start your own New Word Log, getting new words from things you read or from the dictionary.

7

Doodle to Inspire Your Mind's Eye

Doodling helps visualization and memory retention. People who doodle "meaningfully" are merely putting on paper some representation of what's going on in their minds. Meaningful doodles (drawings, sketches, or figures) are those that somehow relate to specific information at hand; they're not an aimless distraction that decreases your attention. Doodles actually enhance visualization and retention because they open up another dimension in how your brain processes information.

If you are listening to the nightly news and want to practice remembering bits of it, keep a drawing pad and pencil at hand. Sketch or doodle whatever comes to mind while listening to the details of the news. A hold-up story might prompt a sketch of a pistol or the front of a convenience store. A 30-point drop in the Dow Jones financial average might suggest something as simple as a downward arrow and "30" falling. Who knows what a story about a newly discovered nude sun-bathing beach might inspire!

Doodling or sketching to aid your memory does not require artistic skill, and it need not be seen by anyone else. If the doodling helps you remember, that's its only purpose.

Making It Work for You

If you are inhibited about doodling, you can learn this skill easily. Along with a blank sheet of paper and a pencil or pen, sit in a quiet place by yourself. Close your eyes and just start doodling. Don't open your eyes for at least five minutes. With your eyes closed, draw whatever comes to mind. Your images will reflect your thoughts, uncensored by your eyes. After a while, open your eyes and look at your doodles. You should be reminded of what you were thinking about when your eyes were closed. With a little practice, you can learn to trust your doodles. You're not doing this to produce a piece of art; you're representing thoughts that you want to remember later.

This sort of doodling helps establish trust in your ability to visually symbolize your memory and rely less on words. We rely so much on words to establish our memories, but nearly half the brain operates on an entirely nonlanguage, visual basis. By practicing doodling you *double* your memory potential.

8

Peg a Thought and Save a Memory

Pegs are key word connections our minds use to conserve brain space. When you say a familiar word such as *terrorist*, a whole string of memories about news stories, movies, airplanes, foreign countries, machine guns, intrigue, face masks, airport security, and so forth comes to mind. A peg word is the mind's label for a memory file. By learning to rely on peg words you can activate a lot of information in your mind linked to a particular word.

To remember the essence of a paragraph you read, pick out the peg word(s)—the fewer the better—that link your visualization and understanding about the information in the paragraph. Once you get in the habit of trusting yourself with peg words, they'll often be all you need to remember the contents of the material linked to them. (Actors and actresses use this technique in learning scripts.) Try it now. What is the peg word in this paragraph? (This one's very easy!) Now tell yourself all you know about this paragraph (without looking at it again) based only on your peg word.

Peg words involve two important aspects of memory: (1) identifying the essential key word most effectively associated with the whole information to be remembered, and (2) trusting your memory that the peg word will be enough to stimulate accurate recall. (If occasionally the peg word is not sufficient, you can go back to the source and relearn the information or add another peg word.)

If you need to learn a lot of new material, consult a memory text that deals with more elaborate techniques for learning to use peg words. "Mind mapping," for example, is a technique that uses both peg words and doodling to draw out a mental map of information. (For further information, see *The Brain Book* by Peter Russell, Hawthorn Books, 1979, or *Mindmapping* by Joyce Wycoff, Berkley Books, 1991.) You also may need to learn how to make sure your learning is complete in the first place so that the peg word actually *is* sufficient to prompt complete recall.

Making It Work for You

Pegs stimulate our thinking and show us we often know more than we think we do. Take a sheet of paper and start writing down all the key words and ideas that come to mind in response to "space travel." (Write "space travel" in the center of the page and add your other words around it, linking them up with lines to show how you mentally connect the words.) You should be able to fill up a sheet of paper with words or short phrases in no time at all. Don't write sentences or tell all you know; just let the peg words flow.

9

Choose Your State of Mind

Absentmindedness is a state (i.e., absence) of mind. Many people consider themselves absentminded because it becomes a convenient excuse for not paying attention. Remember, memory is as efficient as you decide it will be. If you use memory failure to your advantage (that is, as an excuse for mental loafing), you have no right to claim a faulty memory. After all, you are making the choices! You're still the one in control, even if it's control of a bad memory.

The "absentminded professor" got his reputation because he developed a highly selective attention and memory system. His academic brilliance cultivated a dependence on paying attention to only a small part of his world, not to the everyday things that most of us remember automatically. Then, too, despite his genius, he also may have never learned some fundamental organizational techniques. Thus, absentmindedness is a choice, not a helpless condition!

Absentmindedness often occurs when we are too busy or too mentally scattered. Ever walk into a room and forget what you went there for? That occurs not because of a faulty memory per se, but because you had your mind on something else. Take things one at a time; pay attention to what you're doing; avoid distractions. Choose to take control of your memory.

Making It Work for You

How many times have you heard teachers and parents say, "Pay attention now"? Learning *how* to energize our attention and focus on what we're doing is a real challenge. One way to learn better "attention paying" is to tell yourself *what* you are going to pay attention *to*. For example, as you are putting laundry into the washing machine you think of a towel you saw earlier in the bathroom. You finish loading the washer and then walk out of the laundry room, shutting off the light and closing the door. You then find yourself in the bathroom wondering why you are there. Pretty soon, if you look around, you might spot the towel that you wanted to add to the laundry, but meanwhile you will have thought how absentminded you are.

This little scenario, and others similar to it, can be avoided. All you have to do is say to yourself something like "I need to go into the bathroom to get that green hand towel I saw on the floor behind the hamper and add it to this wash." Saying this out loud, right away, energizes your attention to the thought. You'll carry out your thought mindfully rather than absentmindfully.

Chronicle Your Life in a Calendar

Using a calendar builds self-reliance. This means *one* calendar—not one in your pocket, one stuck to the refrigerator, another at the office, and so on. Use a single calendar to record meetings, appointments, assignments, deadlines, tasks and responsibilities, dinner engagements, goals and objectives—virtually every important event in your day-to-day activities. You can even write down things you want to remember that happened that day, even though these things are not "appointments."

Your calendar must be accessible. Use one that you can carry easily and handily, and keep a pen or pencil with it, too. Make sure it has space enough to record lots of things for each day. (One with a whole page per day may be best.) Keep the calendar open to the current day and in a conspicuous place even when you are not writing in it. Refer to it several times a day. Your calendar becomes an extension of your brain's memory cells. (Therefore, make it just yours; don't let others record in it.)

Never regret using a calendar or consider it a cover-up for a bad memory. We set ourselves up to fail when we think that a technique such as using a calendar is an admission of failure or a weakness. If you've never had to use a calendar in the past but can't remember things without one now, that's okay. Don't look back; use whatever techniques you need to use to improve your memory *now*.

Keep and use a fairly detailed daily calendar. As long as you use it regularly (not just occasionally), you will never miss another appointment, birthday, TV show, party, interview, business contact, luncheon, or school assignment. Faithful and complete use of a calendar will reward your confidence many times over. You will feel more secure and organized, which is a much better feeling than the frustration of forgetting things or resentment for "having" to use a calendar.

Making It Work for You

Buy a personal organizer/planner. Carry it with you or have it nearby all the time. Write in it often, as soon as you think of something that needs to be recorded (for later remembering). Some well-known planner systems include Franklin Planner, Time Design, Day-At-A-Glance, Day-Timer, and so forth. Visit an office supply store and select the best tool for your personal needs.

If you are not accustomed to using a personal calendar/planner to manage your time (and memory), it may take some getting used to. Various publishers of planner systems offer courses and texts to help you learn. One current book on successful time management is *The 10 Natural Laws of Successful Time and Life Management* by Hyrum W. Smith (Warner Books, 1994).

11

Accentuate the Positive

Remember the little engine that could? Well, take a lesson from it and stay positive. Avoid negative words like *can't;* they condition you to think about yourself in terms of failures. A comment like "I can't remember all that!" is helpless and defeating right from the start. It sets up a negative self-expectation. We *do* what we believe we can do.

Be the little engine that can. Whenever you get the feeling you can't do something, stop and think how you *can* do it. Instead of saying "I can't remember that," say "I *can* remember that if I write it down and review it a few times." This implies self-control, not self-defeat.

Other kinds of negative thoughts also can make your memory suffer: "That will be too hard," "I'm too stupid," "My memory is not good enough," or "I won't be able to . . . ." Think of ways for turning each of these negative statements into positive ones reflecting that *you* are in control and are positive about yourself. A positive statement might need to include a comment about the mechanism you will use to accomplish your goal. "I can't" implies defeat and no self-control at all, but "I *can* if I do (this and that)" implies confidence and self-control. "I *can*" implies you are taking charge of yourself. No luck or wishes involved here—just sheer determination *and* a specific strategy to make it work for you.

For example, if you think you're not smart enough to learn (and remember) algebra, that's because you are immediately overwhelmed about what algebra is. Just learning that "$3 + x = 5$, $x = 2$" is a start. Now you know the beginnings of algebra. Not so bad, is it? Take things one step at a time, commit to the time necessary to learn, and you can learn just about anything! If you understand the idea behind "$3 + x = 5$, $x = 2$," then you *do* understand algebra, and you can learn some more algebra concepts, one step at a time.

Never make a negative statement about your memory to someone else. Every time you tell someone you think your memory is weak, or bad, or faulty, or gone, or that you're getting old, you reinforce that belief in yourself. Negative self-comments are stronger than positive ones. Therefore, never saying negative statements about yourself means *never*. Language is powerful and how we use it conditions our mind and our behavior. Every time we make a statement about ourselves, we believe and live out that statement a little more strongly.

Although some might argue that this memory tip is an exercise in self-deception, we can, and do, choose to think about ourselves from several different aspects or attitudes. If we choose to make positive statements about ourselves, we will eventually begin to exhibit behaviors that validate the statements.

Making It Work for You

Work on catching yourself (or enlist help from someone else) when you say "can't." Re-frame your thought in some positive terms using the word *can*, not *can't*.

Find a Place for Everything

The adage "A place for everything and everything in its place" works as well for the mind as it does for the kitchen. Being organized helps your memory function better. By feeling that your life and activities are orderly, and at least somewhat predictable, you will feel less scattered or chaotic. Order lets you place new information in your mind where it belongs instead of trying to remember things haphazardly and in a disconnected way.

Most of our lives consist of "areas" of activity: work, family, entertainment, hobbies, financial responsibilities, and so forth. If you have a sense of what category you are living and working in at any given time, you'll more intuitively place new information in that category. For example, some students attempt to study while watching television, combining schoolwork with passive entertainment. Mixing the two, however, interferes with attention and concentration and potentially produces confused learning.

Here's another example: A specific place and time to pay bills will get the job done more accurately and you will remember what you've done. Placing your checkbook and monthly bills in a box or file, keeping the checkbook register up-to-date, and setting up separate files for paid bills and for due bills will make you feel organized. When you work within that organized activity, you will not forget to pay bills, you will have a good sense of the continuity of your budget, and you will feel on top of things. Anything done haphazardly makes your mind feel disorganized.

Making It Work for You

Think of one place you can add a sense of order to your life: a closet, dresser drawers, kitchen, garage, briefcase or purse, workshop, desk. Write down how you could *logically* improve the order and organization of that place, then do it. In general, organizing your life greatly adds to confidence and efficiency, as well as to learning and memory.

If you have the tendency (and the cash) to be an organizational junkie, visit an office supply superstore or a shop that specializes in organizers and containers. You'll be surprised at the variety of wire baskets, cardboard boxes, plastic bins, wooden containers, acrylic receptacles, cloth bags, and other repositories you can find.

13

Jazz Up Your Learning and Memory

Approaching a situation negatively, suspiciously, resentfully, or even passively immediately puts you at a great disadvantage for learning and remembering. Such attitudes interfere with how your memory system stores information accurately. Instead, get yourself positively excited and jazzed up about learning and remembering. If you are excited, your interest will be piqued, and you *will* remember.

High motivation and self-confidence are keys to success in almost all we do. Approach anything with enthusiasm, interest, and energetic involvement and the task is half conquered! If you aren't positive and charged up about learning and remembering—from remembering someone's name to taking in lots of new information at school or the office—the task will be just that much more difficult and incomplete. (Excitement fuels attention, and attention is essential for learning and remembering.)

Emotion is a great motivator for anything. In fact, the emotional system of your brain is closely associated with the memory system. Your brain shares some of the same cells it uses in memory with those it uses in experiencing emotions. Anything that carries strong emotions will likely be remembered very well for a long, long time.

If you can't seem to get jazzed up about learning and re-membering, maybe you need to take a look at your mo-tives. Perhaps your lack of enthusiasm suggests a more basic problem that you might need some help with and in-sight about. Or, maybe you're falling back into a negative expectation pattern and simply need to pep-talk yourself out of it or start using some affirmations again.

Making It Work for You

If you ever feel stuck while trying to learn, do something silly, creative, or unusual to heighten your interest or in-volvement in whatever you are learning. Make jokes, find something uncommon in it, figure out (or make up) how your entire future depends on this learning. It makes no difference how you do this as long as you get yourself even a little more involved with the material. It's always easier to learn and remember things you are caught up with and interested in.

Link New Learning With Old Habits

Old habits are memories; use them to your advantage. When you want or need to pick up a new routine, consciously link old and new habits together. You will remember to do a new task (such as taking medicine in the morning) by linking it with an old habit (such as brushing your teeth when you get up). This is similar to the principle of associations (see tip 30). Why should you have to remember to do two or three separate things when you can join them together and remember to do only one, based on one old habit?

To remember to take your morning medicine, put the container inside the cup you use when you brush your teeth. You'll never forget to take the pills again. If you take them at bedtime instead (or as well), keep a bottle of pills sitting on your alarm clock. By consciously thinking of ways to link things we do (or want to remember to do) with other things we already do by habit, we will simplify our lives—and we *will* remember.

To remember to write in your journal or diary every day, always keep the journal on your bed pillow. Remember to water your plants by keeping a decorative watering can plainly visible next to the plants. Remember to do something special by attaching a note to the handle of your refrigerator or coffeemaker (something you always touch each morning, by habit). Be creative; you'll find potential links in much of your daily routine.

Identify any task that you are not consistent in remembering, and link it to something you are consistent in doing regularly. Often tasks that don't need to be done daily are those more likely to be forgotten. Make some aspect of the task a daily habit. Make a list of all those things you might forget and review the list once a day, asking yourself if each task needs to be done that day. Or, set aside one day each week or month to run through a list (e.g., pay rent, change oil in the car, groom the dog, call Mom, make savings deposit, and so forth). Every time you think you might forget something new, think about something old you can link it up with.

Making It Work for You

Identify something you're sometimes afraid you will forget. Now be creative—what link to something you do habitually can you come up with that will ensure your never forgetting again? Here are some examples of things people often report that they are afraid of forgetting: turning off a stove burner after removing a pot, locking their keys in the car, taking something essential to school or work, or giving the dog a medication he has to take only once a month. How can any of these be linked to already established habits?

15

Find Your Mental Comfort Zone

When you push your mental limits beyond what you can comfortably do or remember, you may feel overloaded. Unfortunately, our culture expects us often to be competitive and to go beyond our native or comfortable level of abilities. Overachievement typically leads to frustration and, ultimately, a sense of failure. Some people who complain the most about their failing memories have been overachievers all their lives, packing in more to do, more to learn and remember, more self-expectations, more responsibility—more, more, more.

Don't feel embarrassed being honest with yourself about what you do and don't feel comfortable doing. Although we often want to improve our functioning (such as our memory), pushing beyond our natural capabilities is destructive. Working on improving ourselves within our natural capabilities is constructive and usually successful.

The "Peter Principle" (Laurence J. Peter, *The Peter Principle*, Bantam, 1970) refers to the individual who is functioning at a level just beyond that which is natural for him or her. Such persons usually collapse from trying to keep themselves in a position in which they don't belong. Failure, poor self-concept, defeat, and weakened physical and mental capabilities typically result.

Work within your level of comfort—whatever that is. You'll feel proud of yourself; you'll do a good job consistently; others will respect you; and all your mental capabilities, including memory, will function naturally and without strain.

Making It Work for You

Think of an example in your own life when you have taken on more than you should have, when you said "yes" but should have said "no." Now, if that situation came up again, how would you handle it differently? How would you avoid the overload and feel good about yourself? One way to say "no" to something to avoid overload is to frame the response within a context that reaffirms your competence but threatens it if you don't say no; for example, "Thanks for asking me to take on this job, but I have to decline the added responsibility. Otherwise, the quality of the work I am already doing will likely suffer. I'd rather do what I'm doing now and do it well than see everything suffer if I take on more than I can handle."

16

Pump Up Your Body and Your Brain

Exercise, relax, and learn. A regular exercise program enhances blood flow and gets nutrients up to the brain. Keeping your brain as physically healthy as possible enhances your memory. Also, exercise relieves stress and tension, a great source of memory distraction, and allows you to relax more fully. Exercise provides added oxygen to the lungs and builds the cardiovascular system that transports oxygen to the brain. Exercise relaxes and clears the mind for re-energizing. It puts you in a more positive frame of mind because it lets your body relax and your mind become freer to learn and remember. Exercise also makes you feel good and minimizes illness, thus keeping your body fit and able to benefit from a good diet, good emotional health, and a positive outlook.

Fatigue, a major culprit in memory problems, is usually relieved by a balance of rest, work, play, and exercise. Regular, but never excessive, exercise often counteracts fatigue by revitalizing and cleansing the body. (Always consult your physician if you have any suspicion of heart, lung, or other physical compromises that may affect how and how often you exercise. And take any exercise program slowly, never working to the point of excessive strain. Get a professionally designed exercise plan that is right for your physical condition and age.)

Fatigue and sleepiness are not the same things. Just because you're fatigued does not mean you're sleepy. We need to know the optimum balance between work and play to minimize fatigue and maximize the benefits of sleep. If you find yourself tired all the time yet unable to sleep much, consult a health professional for assistance. You may need to examine several factors, including disease, too little exercise, mental stress, or some other health problem. A healthy body and a healthy mind go hand in hand.

Making It Work for You

Attend a professionally sponsored exercise class—even for a little while—where you will learn effective and safe techniques. Visit a YMCA, a hospital-sponsored health and wellness program, a fitness club, or a specialty program such as those for senior adults, women, or business executives.

17

Talk Around a Word Block

When you get stuck finding a word to express something you're thinking of, think *around* it. Everyone experiences word-finding blocks now and then. This is where you know the word you want to use but can't actually think of it or say it. You feel blocked and frustrated because you seem out of control of your own thinking. This experience is fairly common and needs to be dealt with immediately, or each recurrence will frustrate you more.

When you experience a block finding a word to express a spoken or written thought, avoid further frustration by immediately starting to think or talk *around* the word. Use similar but not-quite-right words. Express, as best you can, a rough definition of the word you want to use. By keeping your mind active instead of locked into the mental block, your memory will usually land on the word you're reaching for. Letting yourself stay stuck on something is like beating your head against a wall. Accept the block as a normal occurrence and encourage yourself to think freely instead of getting down on yourself. The word will come to you eventually or you'll become satisfied with another one.

When we are engaged intently in describing or writing about something, it is not at all unusual to experience a word block. That is because our brains are hard at work making a lot of connections and forming a lot of associations. The exact association you want may get lost temporarily in the maze of mental connections. Give it time. Help yourself out by talking or thinking around the word you're searching for.

Making It Work for You

Here's a little game you can play with your spouse, kids, or friends. Think of a word, then give the other person(s) clues to the word you are thinking of. The clues should be obscure enough to stump them but reasonably accurate, too. This game forces your brain to think *around* something. It will prime you to start thinking with rich word links.

There are at least 10 billion nerve cells in the human brain, each of which may have hundreds or even thousands of connections with other cells. As Richard Restak writes in *The Brain* (Bantom Books, 1984), "The total number of connections within the brain's neural system is truly astronomical—greater than the number of particles in the known universe." Learning to optimize the richness of these links in the brain is the task of all learning and remembering. The richer the links, the more flexible the thinking.

18 Tell the Truth and Always Know What the Truth Is

Never make up something to cover up not remembering. If you don't recall the details of something right away, be sensitive to what you *are* recalling as fact versus what you *think* you are recalling as fact. If you're not sure, check it out rather than assume anything.

Fabrication can become a habit. And when you make up little details about something you're trying to remember, the little lies will eventually catch up. The result will be that you (and others) will not trust you, you will get frustrated, and people will correct (or doubt) your "facts." The next time you tell someone something but have some doubt about its accuracy, admit that you aren't sure. Or, better yet, get your facts straight before relating them to anyone else.

Often, fabricating is almost unconscious. When we share information with others, we are driven to be as coherent and complete as possible. And if we forget some detail, we often make up something to fill in. Although this may be totally unconscious, if you become sensitive to when you are uncertain about something, you can admit your uncertainty and then go about finding out the real facts.

Remember the party game where one person tells a brief story to another person, then that person tells the story to a third, that person tells it to a fourth, and so on? The story gets changed and usually embellished with each retelling. This is unintentional fabrication. Something about the story wasn't heard correctly or was forgotten, so something else had to be made up to make the story "hang together." Outside a party, in real life, we need to be sensitive to that information which we know is accurate versus that which we suspect we may know inaccurately or incompletely.

Making It Work for You

One of the major television network news shows carries a segment called "Reality Check" that's designed to sort fact from fiction in the news. It's a good idea to develop your own personal reality check. Sometimes what we read, hear, and pass on to others is of marginal accuracy. There is no need to perpetuate inaccuracy—this only clutters your mind and interferes with accurate recall. Cultivate the sound of a little bell going off in your mind when you need to stop and do a reality check on something you have doubts about. Then seek to clarify things in your own mind. You'll remember accurately the information you feel sure about.

19

Forgive Yourself— Memory Glitches Are Normal

Everyone forgets things once in a while. When you think your memory has failed you, *never* get angry or hate yourself for it. Instead, repeat an affirmation, such as "We all make mistakes and forget things, but I am concentrating more now to remember things as well as I can, and I am learning and using the techniques to do so."

This affirmation does not create undue expectations; rather, it helps cultivate a trust in yourself that you can achieve by adopting a positive and self-respecting mental set. Getting down on yourself when you forget something or when you take longer than you think you should to learn something only feeds your mind's negativity. Accept that you are human, that you make mistakes, and that you *do* occasionally forget things. (Of course, you're also interested in minimizing the incidences of forgetting things, and by practicing the tips in this book you will do absolutely that.)

Some people do forget more than others do or more than they themselves used to (because of a brain injury, for example). But, you can't improve your memory by always comparing it with someone else's, or with how it used to be, or with how you think it should be. You are who and what you are *today*. You'll never be who and what you were yesterday. You can become who and what you want tomorrow—as long as you let your self-confidence, self-trust, self-acceptance, and commitment determine your future. Unrealistic expectations are founded on lack of self-confidence and self-acceptance. Trust yourself, believe in yourself, and accept yourself. Be human!

Making It Work for You

Some people confuse an affirmation with a wish. These are not at all the same things: A wish does not imply control. An affirmation is based on the premise that you *are* in control of your beliefs and your deeds. Consider an affirmation you can use that directly states *how* you are in control of your memory, how you are training your memory, and how you are committed to making the training work for you. Write out and revise your affirmation as necessary until it feels right for you.

Outline the Essence of What You Want to Remember

Create an outline to pull the essence from new information you are tackling. Anything can be outlined, from lectures to a daily activity schedule. An outline functions much like a hierarchical list. By going to the heart of the new information and making the outline yourself, essential phrases or words in an organized structure will be sufficient to jog your memory. An outline resembles an organized list of peg words (see tip 8).

Outlines, like doodling, are personal. They need not be seen by others and, hence, need only contain the key information you need to function. Be judicious, succinct, terse, essential! Resist the temptation to outline in sentence form; use only key words to cue your memory about a specific fact or idea. Include drawings, sketches, and doodles in your outline if you like. Order and meaning (to you) is more important than neatness.

Outlining a lecture, a radio or television newscast, or some other auditory information requires that you listen actively for key words. Information that is moving fast must be reduced to its essence quickly. Alternatively, if you are outlining something you yourself are going to speak about later, you'll have more time to think now than when you're on the speaker's podium. Get your thoughts down on paper as fast as they flow. By outlining, you can go back and add the necessary ideas, words, and embellishments to make sentences later. Your outline should be composed of key words (pegs) and phrases (with drawings, sketches, and doodles) instead of complete sentences or unnecessary words.

Making It Work for You

Outlining may seem a little intimidating at first, but you'll be surprised how easy it actually is. With a pad of paper and a pen, sit down to watch a half-hour news program on television. Outline the essence of the news using only a two-level structure: A, B, C, and so on for the key word or phrase of each story, then 1, 2, 3 for the points under each story. Don't forget to doodle if you wish.

21

Synergize Your Learning Using All Your Senses

Learning by using all your senses and modalities makes storing information in memory much easier. While we usually rely on verbal and visual learning, the sense of touch and the sense of movement can offer added opportunities for memory storage, using the brain areas related to these additional senses. Be aware of what things feel or smell like, or how heavy or light they are. By attending to such details, the memory created will be more vivid and, hence, strengthened.

You can enhance your memory of being in a special place if you pay attention to how you *feel* being there, what the air smells like, the touch of objects in the place, and the sense of heat or cold on your hands and feet and face. Take it all in and you will remember much better. Plus the memory will be alive, making it easier to relive.

When learning to perform a specific task, pay attention to how it *feels* to do it. This involves both touch and the sense of what your muscles are doing while performing the task. Even something as simple as a new telephone number can be learned more easily if you attend both to the order of pushing the buttons as well as to what it feels like with each finger pushing those buttons in the correct sequence. (The pattern of tones you hear also becomes part of the memory.)

By attending to multiple sensory information, you are paying attention to details and how those details fit together. The more types of information you put into your brain about something, the more easily you will learn it and remember it later. Remember, you can't overload the brain as long as all the information going in "hangs together."

Making It Work for You

Find something you want to remember (an unusual word or name, for example). Now do each of these things in succession: See it—*really* see it, every letter. Now spell it out loud, letter by letter. Now spell it phonetically. Take it slowly. Now say the name out loud. Now write it. Now associate a sense of the "feel" about the word or name. Is it hard or soft, rough or smooth? Does the word conjure any sense of smell? Any visual sensation? Synergy is the uniting of senses into a dynamic whole. What better way to excite your memory system?

22

Unblock Your Memory and Free Your Thinking

Examine inner conflicts that might block your memory. Become aware of something specific you have had trouble remembering (names, formulas, instructions, appointments, work responsibilities, things your spouse tells you, or whatever), then lie down and think hard about it. Ask yourself, "What conflict within me is causing this memory block?"

This technique poses a real challenge. If it were that easy to become aware of our mental blocks and do something about them, we wouldn't need psychologists. But at least by giving yourself the time and energy to do some soul searching, you might stir up some insights. Conflict and a negative attitude about something or someone are often the root causes of memory blocks. You block the memory of things you subconsciously don't want to remember. And that subconscious block is usually rooted in some kind of conflict.

For example, sometimes students do poorly in a class because they have a negative block about the subject matter, the instructor, or being coerced into taking the class against their will. Their failure to remember has little to do with their competency or lack thereof in learning and remembering. It stems from a conflict that is very powerful in blocking learning. If you are having exceptional trouble remembering your marriage anniversary, showing up for important meetings, following through with assignments from your boss, or paying your analyst's bill, perhaps there's a mental block there. Something deep-seated in your mind is causing you to forget because your subconscious mind does not want you to remember.

If you need extra help, seek a therapist to assist you. Often memory problems are really deeply hidden emotional conflicts. These conflicts are psychological and have nothing directly to do with faulty memory nerves in the brain. If you want to remember things well, get rid of the emotional baggage that is keeping you from a better, and freer, memory.

Making It Work for You

If you sense some conflict (or anger, or resentment) about something in your life, figure out how and when that conflict might be a barrier to your learning and remembering. What can you do to eliminate, or at least minimize, the conflict?

23

Write Down What's Important in Your Life

J ust the act of writing something down greatly improves your ability to spontaneously remember it later. Whether you are a homemaker, business person, student, or retiree, getting in the habit of regularly formulating your thoughts and writing them down can provide a sense of mental organization and continuity in your life. Writing is how we learned to learn way back in kindergarten, and it still works.

To keep a journal or a diary, write in a special notebook (not your daily calendar) your thoughts, ideas, lists, and anything else you want to remember that is not specifically date-dependent. Writing things down provides a visual sense of "connectedness" to your thoughts and feelings. It also forces clearer thinking because in order to translate ideas into words, you have to organize the ideas and put them into concrete form—words on paper.

When you think of something you want to remember, the part of your brain that stimulated the thought is probably relatively small. But if you write down the thought, you stimulate multiple brain areas, thus enhancing your brain's association pathways for remembering. The act of writing activates the part of your brain that controls your pen or pencil in response to your mental commands, plus when your eyes see what you have written, this activates additional brain areas. You have just tripled the brain area that processed those original thoughts! With a mental, visual, and even muscular experience of your thoughts, you'll remember them much easier.

Select at least one time each day to write. Start with just a sentence or two. Within a few days you'll be writing a lot, and remembering a lot, too. It's especially valuable to write when you want to remember something as vividly as possible for many years. The memory of a trip to a special place or a meeting with a special person will be heightened if you journal the experience.

Making It Work for You

Many bookstores sell "blank books," attractive bound volumes of various sizes that just contain blank or lined pages. Selecting such a book can inspire permanence and special contents (your personal thoughts). Visit a bookstore and select a blank book with a cover that says "you," and use it to start your journal collection.

24

Plan Ahead and Avoid Chaos

Planning facilitates learning and memory; chaos interferes with both. If you think of something you have to take to the office in the morning, put it by the door immediately. If you need certain materials to accomplish a job, collect and organize them first, before you dig into the job. These are simple examples of planning ahead. When you think ahead, you will be more organized, be less apt to become confused, feel more in control of a task, accomplish it more quickly and efficiently, and not be as prone to forgetting some detail and becoming frustrated about it. Planning ahead also slows down your thinking, so forgetting a step later on is less likely.

Planning a trip, an agenda for a meeting, an outline for a report, a day's activities, a special home project, or whatever you have ahead of you will provide a foundation on which all the details, facts, and images can fall into place. Building a set of mental pigeon-holes first is like setting up a filing system for an office. Things will run much more smoothly if there is a place in your brain predesignated for new information. Writing down the plan is important, too.

So many people start off on things "half-cocked." This is a sure-fire reason they don't finish projects, don't remember what to do next, or become confused and disillusioned. If you aren't organized and don't have a good plan, you'll find yourself backtracking, forgetting things you need, and getting frustrated with yourself. Remember the adage, "If you don't use your head, you'll have to use your feet."

You can see how planning relates integrally to memory. As you know by now, memory is very dependent on how we learn and think in the first place. Planning ahead is just one more means of becoming organized so that you *can remember* later.

Making It Work for You

Think of a task you don't do very often (preparing a unique food, constructing storage shelves, planting a tree). Write down, in numbered order, every step required to accomplish the task. Be very detailed. From that plan you can then extract a materials list as well as estimate the time needed for each step and the overall project. Use this technique the next time you undertake any special job or activity.

Planning ahead has as much to do with memory as remembering the past does. As the Queen remarked in *Alice's Adventures in Wonderland*, "It's a poor sort of memory that only works backwards." Thinking ahead as well as behind provides a sense of continuity to our memory and helps us feel organized.

25

Sequence the Sands of Time

As time passes, the things you do become linked together in your personal time line. You can facilitate recollection by reconstructing the sequence of events associated with whatever it is you want to recall. When you can't remember the date or some other details of a past event, make a written or mental list of happenings that surrounded the event you are attempting to recall. One dimension that our brains use to store information is reference to a timeframe. By reconstructing a timeframe you are regenerating the natural links that your brain has made to the information you are attempting to recall.

If you want to remember when you last had your car's oil changed (because you didn't keep a written record of it like you should have), start thinking of what you can remember about the day you had the work done: where you took the car for service, what the weather was like, the conversation you had with the service attendant, why you happened to choose that time and day (was it right before you left on a trip?), other work that was done, what you might have done before or after you had the car serviced, and so forth. When was the last time you visited a certain relative or friend that you don't see too often? Recalling as many characteristics as you can about the visit will help you reconstruct a timeframe. Once you link up memories in this manner, many other associated memories will gradually surface into awareness more easily.

A sense of the passage of time and of the sequence of events linked to that passage of time is important for establishing and recalling continuity in one's life. Practice recalling what you were doing a month ago, or reconstruct how long it's been, for example, since you visited your dentist. This will help you maintain memory continuity.

Making It Work for You

Continuity of time—months, seasons, years, and decades—is fundamental to how we think about things, especially events. Becoming more aware of *when* you do things will help your brain register the activity or event within a time continuity sense. At least mentally recording the sense of time that accompanies events will help you remember them later. Of course, keeping a journal of your life's special events and thoughts as well as a daily calendar will help, too!

26

Sticky Notes Jog Memories

Sticky notes (small sheets with a tacky strip across the back) are great for writing quick reminders. Jot something down, stick it almost anywhere, then remove it easily and throw it away when it has served its purpose. Keep a pad of these notes on your nightstand, at your desk, by the phone—almost anywhere you might suddenly need to make yourself a reminder.

Use sticky notes judiciously. They can be placed in crucial spots—on the dash of your car, the door you pass through when you leave the house, the telephone, and so forth. Make sure that wherever you put the note, it's the most relevant place for it. (Don't put the note to call a friend or client on your dash, unless of course you intend to call from the phone in your car.) And once the note has done its job, immediately throw it away.

Get in the habit of using these notes. If you need to remember to get gas in the car but are afraid you'll forget the next time you go out, write "GAS" on the sticky note and go to the garage and put it on the steering wheel *now*. If you need to ask your friend something when she calls later, put a sticky note on the handle of the phone. If you need to remind yourself to do something in the morning, put a sticky note right in the middle of the mirror in your bathroom.

Using these handy reminders is not an admission of a bad memory. It is a strategy that works wonders *for* your memory. Getting in the habit of using such memory aids makes life so much easier because you are not getting down on yourself for forgetting things. You are being *responsible* for remembering.

Making It Work for You

Sticky notes are like Velcro: They have endless uses, and it can be a challenge to see how many ways they can make our life more efficient. Buy packs of them, perhaps in different sizes and colors, and turn them into "flags for thoughts."

27

Praise Yourself for Your Good Work

Reward yourself when you've remembered something well, but never punish yourself for a memory "failure." Rewards generate self-confidence and lay the groundwork for an efficient memory in the future. Although we're usually quick to condemn and berate ourselves and notice our shortcomings, positive reinforcement goes much further in establishing success. Positive reward reinforces the idea that we're on the right track. Punishment says we're "wrong" but doesn't give us any sense of what is right.

Rewarding yourself with positive thoughts (or a pat on the back, or even a candy bar) when you remember something helps maintain a positive attitude. Just as we are quick to point out faults in others before we notice their strengths, we do the same within ourselves. If you maintain an awareness of the good (both in others and in yourself) and try to ignore the bad, eventually you'll be quite good all the time!

Making It Work for You

The idea of a positive attitude and giving yourself due credit for recognizing a positive attitude is powerful medicine. It can be fun to establish a reinforcement system for yourself. Get a jar full of little candies like M&Ms. Every time you become aware of a memory success, however trivial, treat yourself. If you get really good at this, go find some sugar-free candy or your self-image may begin to suffer for other reasons!

If you are facing a particularly troubling block in your life and want to learn more in-depth methods for self-modification and self-reinforcement, read "Self-control Procedures in Personal Behavior Problems." This classic self-help article by I. Goldiamond (*Psychological Reports*, 1965, volume 17, pages 851-868) on the use of systematic desensitization and other conditioning techniques goes beyond the scope of this particular memory tip. However, it focuses on the idea that we can learn a variety of strategies to strengthen positive behavior—our good works—and diminish our negative behaviors. An occasional reward with an M&M *does* work to strengthen our sense of self-control and to reinforce the kinds of behavior we *want*. Slightly more sophisticated techniques, as offered by Goldiamond, can be useful for more demanding self-modification.

28

Teach in Order to Learn

Talk yourself through learning and remembering. Doing so is like teaching someone else, and one of the best ways to learn is to teach. If you need to remember a new procedure at work, for example, talk your way through it the first few times as if you were teaching a co-worker. Talking about what you are doing reinforces concentration and provides an added mode of "encoding" what you are doing into your brain.

This technique also works well for other situations where your primary aim is not specifically to remember something. Putting something together (like a piece of assemble-it-yourself furniture, a toy, or a bicycle) can be intimidating and frustrating. Take the printed instructions one step at a time and talk your way through everything. This will keep your mind focused on the order of operations and will force you to take things step-by-step. Talking out loud and following your own commands slows your thinking down to a comfortable pace.

Sometimes even just reading aloud helps us conceptualize, understand, and remember something. If we read something, only a small part of our brain is energized (the visual pathways). If we also *say* what we are reading, we increase the areas of the brain involved in understanding threefold (the reading or visual part, the expressive language or talking part, and the receptive language or listening to ourselves part).

If you are really intent on learning something well, learn it first as best you can, then find a way to actually teach it to others. Community colleges, local parks and recreation departments, senior centers, and so forth are always looking for people to teach new skills.

Making It Work for You

Come up with something (a knowledge, special talent, or hobby) that is special to you and a unique part of your life. Now, think of some way you can share this specialness with others. Whenever you teach someone about something you know a lot about, you reinforce your own knowledge. But a side benefit of teaching is that you also become aware of holes or weaknesses in your skill or knowledge. You can then undertake your own knowledge expansion to fill those holes and strengthen your competence.

29

Chunk Little Bits of Information

Learning and remembering is often achieved effectively through "chunking." This technique simply involves grouping information in "bite-size" portions. Put new information into appropriate categories; find common properties that link ideas and facts together; identify similar functions or processes; and don't bite off more than you can chew.

Often we feel intimidated by new learning and recall because we can't handle the whole enchilada. Find ways to break down a learning and remembering task into small segments that somehow make sense. If you are recalling information from something you read, for example, start with one main idea, a peg word, or a visualization. Identify that recollection as chunk number one. Think about it a while and something else will pop into memory. Identify that recollection as chunk number two. Pretty soon the memories will start to fall into place. While the memory may never be complete, chunking will help your recall if you've failed to journal the information or you weren't using other memory enhancement techniques at the time you first learned the information.

Another, and obvious, use of chunking occurs in learning numbers. If you need to learn the phone number 734-6182, don't try to learn it by memorizing 7, 3, 4, 6, 1, 8, 2. Chunk it in natural segments. Take the prefix, seven hundred thirty-four, then follow with sixty-one, and then eighty-two. Instead of learning seven numbers, you only have to learn three. It is easier to visualize chunks, too. You can "see" in your mind "61" and "82" easier than the string "6, 1, 8, 2."

Making It Work for You

For practice in chunking, think of last Tuesday. Sit back and recall all you can about it. Start with any memory of that day that comes up. Identify this as a distinct memory and associate whatever you can with it. Whenever something else pops up about last Tuesday, think of that as another more-or-less distinct memory, too. You can take this as far as you like, and you'll be surprised how well it works. Given enough associations (and chunks of memory), you'll likely remember what you were wearing, what you did, what you had for lunch, and so forth.

30

Associate Ideas to Form Mental Links

The starting point for memory is association. Unconsciously, our minds learn (and later remember) by associating new learning with old learning. That's the biological way our brains work. You can facilitate this natural mechanism by making it a more conscious process.

Almost anything you want to remember can be linked to something you already know and with which you are already familiar. The richer and more varied our associations of knowledge, the easier it is to remember anything. Information naturally gets associated with other information instead of existing in our brains in isolation. Creativity is also stimulated as we enrich the associations among the knowledge we already have.

When you hear something you want to remember, immediately associate it with something you think of spontaneously. The name of a foreign country, for example, can be associated with something, however obscure, that you already know about the country. Or you can associate it with the sound of some other word that's similar. Or try visualizing something about that country that will remind you of its name. Your spontaneous imagination is all that's needed, but make it *conscious*. Learning that is active is well retained. Consciously thinking of links makes learning that much stronger—and memorable.

When your learning is enthusiastic, positive, involved, and active, your brain naturally and effortlessly forms new and richly varied association links. See how these memory pointers are all beginning to link together?

Making It Work for You

Select a short newspaper or magazine article. Read it slowly, sentence by sentence. Stop at the end of each sentence and ask yourself the question, "What does this sentence make me think of that I already know or remember?" This kind of practice will help build your natural curiosity and will enrich your learning—and memory.

31

Concentrate on What You're Doing

Distraction is the foremost thief of learning and memory. Therefore, don't do anything important until you can concentrate on it. Being preoccupied and distracted interferes with learning and memory; it results in absent-mindedness. If you have to get a report done or study for a test, do it only when you can make the most of your time and give it your undivided attention. If you are worried, thinking about something else, or want to do something else first, you probably won't be efficient at the task you think you should be doing.

Whenever you do anything, *think* of what you are doing at that moment. Make sure your mind is present, not absent. A common area where concentration is necessary is in remembering people's names. This is a real problem for many of us often because we're not really concentrating on the person in the first place. When introduced to someone, immediately focus on him or her by noticing eye color, face shape, hair color, and so forth. Mentally (at least) say the name back to yourself. Be impressed with the person you want to know and remember. Say something flattering. These techniques get the focus and concentration where it belongs—on the other person. If you are preoccupied with yourself, you will probably forget the name of the person to whom you were just introduced because your focus of concentration was not on him or her.

If you need to read a technical manual or something similarly demanding, do it only when you can concentrate.

And let your natural concentration be your guide. If you find that your mind wanders after just 10 minutes, then you know that 10 minutes is your maximum concentration time for that particular task. Take a break, then go back to it. If you fight a concentration problem, you won't learn and remember anyway, and you'll build up a real negativity toward the material you're attempting to concentrate on, learn, and remember.

Making It Work for You

The next time you leave your house, stop at the door before you exit. Say to yourself something like, "I'm leaving the house now. I've turned off the lights; I've checked the doors and windows to make sure they are locked; I turned down the thermostat; and I am locking this door behind me." If you worry about whether you've done something important, make the task conscious instead of unconscious.

32

Eat Your Way to a Healthy Memory

Proper nutrition is often overlooked as a significant contribution to memory proficiency. The brain benefits from all the vitamins, minerals, and proteins that the rest of your body requires. If any part of the body—liver, heart, lungs, nerves, glands—isn't functioning up to par, the brain will suffer. While the brain directs all your bodily functions, it relies on the rest of the body for its own health and well-being.

Your brain needs lots of glucose and oxygen to work at its peak. The body manufactures glucose from the foods you eat, and then healthy blood carries it along with oxygen to the brain. It isn't necessary to be fanatical—and certainly not faddish—about diet. If you need a special diet because of obesity, diabetes, or some other condition, follow your health-care professional's advice. Otherwise, a basically healthy person can easily achieve a balanced diet every day by consuming a variety of proteins, vegetables, grains, and fruits. Reducing your fat and sugar intake can help maintain proper weight and keep the blood vessels open. Cultivating a broad interest in nutritional issues and heeding that awareness will provide the healthy foundation for using your brain to its maximum.

There is a corollary to keeping the brain healthy through a good diet. You can prevent ill health of your brain by avoiding too much alcohol, nonprescription drugs, and cigarettes. Alcohol interferes with your blood's ability to transport oxygen; many drugs interfere with the brain's information transmitters; and cigarettes reduce your lungs' capacity to absorb oxygen.

In addition to maintaining good nutrition and avoiding body contaminants, keep the blood flowing freely throughout your body. Don't wear tight neckwear or other constrictive clothing. A chronically tight collar will gradually restrict the blood flowing to your brain through the carotid arteries. Let your oxygen- and glucose-rich blood flow freely!

Making It Work for You

If you feel your knowledge of basic nutrition is weak, check out a book on the topic from your public library. Or visit a health food store or a bookstore to find some literature on maintaining a healthy diet. Take stock of your eating habits and, if necessary, write out a plan to modify your diet. Don't cut down on balanced food to lose weight. If weight is a problem, consult a professional for advice so you don't compromise your brain's needs by eliminating nutritional foods. If you need to reverse years of unhealthy habits, read *Reversing Memory Loss* by Vernon H. Mark and Jeffrey P. Mark (Houghton Mifflin, 1992).

33

Take It Easy and Be Patient

Be patient with yourself when you aren't as speedy as you'd like in recalling something. Life is not a rapid-fire TV game show where you have to come up with the answer in five seconds. Every time you become frustrated with yourself for not immediately recalling something, you put new pressure and stress on yourself that will inhibit memory in the future. Give yourself a break.

Many times we get frustrated with ourselves or even embarrassed if we can't think of a person's name, remember the title of a movie or book, or recall some trivial bit of information. Frustration blocks memory just that much more. Relax. Sometimes your brain needs time to work through all those circuits up there. Give yourself the time—kindly. Remember, only an infinitesimal fraction of people have the lightning-fast memories that get you a spot on "Jeopardy."

Never say "I can't think of that." Instead, say "I am not thinking of that right now, but I will think of it in a while." This is positive, and it implies that you are taking control of your memory and letting it work *with* you instead of *against* you. While you may not think of the specific thing you want to recall right now, give yourself the opportunity to think of it a little later. And relax! If you remain relatively frustration free, your memory *will* work with you.

If you want to recall the name of someone you are thinking about, go slowly through the alphabet and visualize each letter to see if that helps your brain circuits make the right connections. Or talk about the person, his or her qualities. The name will come to you when your brain is ready to make the link. Remember that your brain is busy process-ing huge amounts of information every second. Rarely does memory fail us if we trust it, give our brain the time it needs, and clear our thoughts to give the mind room to think effectively.

Making It Work for You

Often we block on recalling something very familiar, such as the name of our best friend, and that's embarrassing. This kind of block usually occurs because we fear it. Write an affirmation that will help you build trust in your mem-ory by relaxing and eliminating memory fears. (Reread memory tip 2.)

34

Say What You See to Remember It

See it—say it—remember it. Saying out loud what you see and want to remember is a potent memory aid. Sometimes just seeing something in writing, even many times, is not sufficient unless you can easily say (or read) it out loud. Verbalizing energizes a whole different set of brain cells than merely looking at something. You can see the printed word *liaison* many times, but until you are comfortable pronouncing it out loud easily and without hesitation, you may not easily remember it (or remember how to spell it) when you need that word.

Mathematical formulas provide another example. You can see a formula such as

$$Amt = P(1 + \frac{r}{n})^{nt}$$

but you will have a difficult time remembering it (much less understanding it) unless you can read it properly. Take the formula from the left side, one element at a time: The amount of the balance (*Amt*) equals the original principal (*P*) multiplied by 1 plus the annual interest rate (*r*) divided by the number of annual compoundings (*n*), all taken to the power of the number of compoundings (*n*) times total years of investment (*t*). Now you can more easily remember the formula for simple interest. One of the problems students have in learning mathematics is that they don't take the time to learn how to read formulas or equations. Just looking at one is usually intimidating, when it really need not be.

A similar situation occurs with proper names. If someone sees the name "Swiercinsky," he or she often blocks and gasps because it looks too complicated. But sounding it out—out loud, letter by letter—makes it very easy to learn *and remember*. "Swear-sin-ski."

If you are cooking from a new recipe, it can be very useful to read through the entire recipe, out loud first, so that you don't forget a step or ingredient. Step-by-step reading slows your thinking down so you can process all the information. It also energizes more brain areas to enhance your concentration and understanding.

Making It Work for You

The next time you want to help yourself remember something you look up in a directory such as the *TV Guide*, put your finger on the line you're looking at and say it out loud. This is more memory-instilling than just reading the line. (Of course, you can also write the information on a sticky note, form a visual image, tie a string around your finger, and toss the *TV Guide* into the middle of the television room!)

35

Become an Expert at Something

An expert possesses specialized knowledge and continues to cultivate it—for as long as he or she wishes to remain an expert. Expertise comes with confidence in your knowledge area and eagerness to learn more. Being an expert establishes you as credible, reliable, and resourceful.

Gaining competence in a topic builds knowledge and memory. The more specialized knowledge and understanding you acquire, the more confident you will become. And, the more confident you become, the better your memory will be—not only in your particular area, but generally.

Anyone who possesses special knowledge, is really excited about it, and can share it with others has to have a good memory. Being an expert and having a good memory reinforce each other. It's not relevant which came first, the memory ability or the knowledge. It's a matter of letting each strengthen the other.

When you increase your knowledge, find ways to apply it, think creatively about it, or share it with others, you are really working those brain cells. The richer the mind, the more positive the spirit, the more confident the self—the better the memory.

Making It Work for You

You probably already are something of an expert in some area or another. If you enjoy a special hobby, have worked or studied in a particular field, or have read a great deal about a specific topic, you are well on the road to being an expert. Now, begin to *think* of yourself as an expert. As long as you commit yourself to being an expert in something, you are obligated to maintain and continuously upgrade your expertise. Read, talk to others with similar interests or knowledge, write, lecture, teach, and perform your special abilities. Establish your standing, seek always to improve it, and see how confident—and memorable—you become.

The more you learn, the more you'll retain; our memory capacity is infinite. As Francis Bacon (*Apothegms*, 1624) reminds us, "Cato said the best way to keep good acts in memory was to refresh them with new." Each new bit of learning in a particular subject helps build one's expert status.

36

Care About What You Learn

If you really care about what you are learning, it will have meaning. Without caring or meaning attached, learning and then remembering won't come easily. If you are unsure about something you want to remember later, whether it's factual information or ideas, ask questions or focus more on the details—get involved, see how the information relates to your life, give it some personal meaning. Sometimes the real reason for a poor performance on a test, for example, is not a faulty memory—it's a failure to care about the topic or the information in the first place.

An effective way to give something meaning and thus to care about it is first to ask yourself some questions that can make the information personal and practical. Teachers, for example, often present stated objectives before introducing new information. These objectives give students specific things to look for during the course of learning. If the objectives relate to a personal need or interest of yours, then the topic and subsequent learning will be more relevant and memorable. If you don't learn something well in the first place (that is, with meaning), you of course won't remember it well later!

Since most of us don't spend much time in the classroom as adults, here's a more familiar example: If your doctor has told you something about a symptom you are having, you won't remember (accurately) much about what he or she told you unless you understand it relatively well. Ask questions, get a pamphlet, take notes, have the doctor draw a diagram—do anything that helps increase *meaningfulness*. Then you'll remember.

When you must glean your information from written material, try the "SQ3R" method of learning. That is, Survey the material, pose Questions (to yourself or to someone else) about the material and how it might relate to your life, Read the material, Recite (to yourself or to someone else) what you have just read, and, finally, Review the material (and the notes you took or outline you made while reading). This technique both helps you find meaning in new learning and enhances your long-term retention.

Making It Work for You

Think of something you were once asked to learn (maybe for a class you had to take—but didn't want to—in school). Reflect on the experience and ask yourself how you might have changed your perception so that you could have cared more about the information and made it more meaningful. In some way, almost everything has relevance to our personal lives if we just look for it.

37

Activate Your Listening to Engage Your Memory

When you're engaged in conversation with someone, be actively (instead of passively) involved. Make frequent eye contact, be aware of your own body posture, look sharp and attentive. (As a bonus, your conversation partner will probably pay better attention to you, too.) While listening, think of a question you can ask back or a comment you can make that reflects you *are* connecting with what the person is saying. Take written notes if appropriate.

If you catch yourself complaining that you don't remember what someone has told you, you probably weren't interested or weren't actively listening in the first place. If you have any negative or resistant thoughts about listening to someone, it's difficult to concentrate and be an active listener. Become aware of the distracting attitudes and thoughts you may harbor that interfere with active listening, then do something about resolving them so you can listen fully.

Sometimes, too, we are so caught up in ourselves—our own beliefs, our own insecurities, our own boastfulness—that we don't stop to really listen to others. Doing so means being able to respond to what they're saying. If something you've heard sparks a thought directly related to what the other person is saying, you are actively listening.

Remember—the person with the great memory knows who's in control of that memory. Don't blame poor memory for what you can take charge of from the start.

Making It Work for You

Is there someone you must listen to that you find boring, or with whom your mind wanders instead of paying attention? Next time find ways to ask questions of that person so that you become engaged with what they are saying.

From lectures to idle conversation, learn to focus (and remember) by becoming involved. This is the essence of what we call "attention." The art of paying attention *is* the art of memory. For any instance that presents itself, figure out some manner of activating your attention. Before entering a lecture or presentation, prime yourself with questions. Plan to make an outline. Circle peg words that you write down. And be sure to doodle.

38

Check and Double-Check What You Learn

Double-check the accuracy of new information you want to remember. Information that's accurate (that is, complete) is more easily accessible to your memory later. Anything inaccurate or incomplete will be stored inaccurately and with erroneous links and associations. Correct input at the start makes your memory system work more efficiently when you need to recall something later.

Putting correct information into the memory system means learning it within the appropriate context and with accurate meaning. Scattered information, irrelevant information, or frankly inaccurate information does not have a solid context "peg" that will enable its reliable recall later. Our minds don't easily store trivia; those people who can usually have a knack for storing that information with elaborate links. Often their stored "trivia" isn't really so at all; it's actually part of some information linked to a broader knowledge base. It only seems like trivia to those around them who don't possess that broader based knowledge.

Business rules, legal regulations, obscure procedures, or facts about anything must be understood in the complete context of why, when, and where they are applied. Memorizing information that is not fairly completely understood, or which cannot be understood in a context, usually becomes very difficult to remember accurately.

Be cautious about forming bizarre visualizations to facilitate learning new information. If the visualization isn't really accurate, many weeks later you may recall the information inaccurately because of imprecise visualization or other inaccurate association. If in doubt, ask questions about the new information to ensure its accuracy before storing it mentally.

Making It Work for You

Learn to question anything that appears as a "fact." Many supermarket tabloids, for example, masquerade as vehicles of facts that are really nothing more than entertaining fabrications. If a "fact" has no credible basis to it, forget it. When you're unsure, check things out through some other source to either verify or dismiss them. Check and double-check what you learn to keep your mind and memory free of clutter.

39

Organize Your Life and Your Mind

A sense of organization greatly enhances your self-confidence and efficiency. You also remember things more easily if the information you need to remember is organized. Even tasks as simple as finding your keys, wallet, remote control, sunglasses, school assignment, address book, pen, calendar, purse, or reading glasses become much easier if each of these things has a specific (and logical) place to be kept *consistently*. When you put one of these objects down, ask yourself if that's where it belongs. If you answer "no," then put it where it does belong, right away. This may be a new habit you'll need to acquire, but one that will save your memory and save you from much aggravation.

Don't put your sunglasses down on the counter when you're in a store; drop them down attached to a chain around your neck or fold them and put them in your shirt pocket. Don't toss your keys just anywhere when you come inside; hang them on their hook by the door or put them in your purse or pocket. Hang your jacket in the closet. Keep your personal things (briefcase, handbag, planner, notebook, and so forth) on your lap when you're in a temporary place (someone else's office, a restaurant, a bus, and so forth). *Never* set anything down in a convenient but unusual place; you'll be more likely to forget it.

Organized living is the key here. Have a definite place for all your belongings—and keep them in their definite place. The place for your wallet is in your hand or in your pocket, absolutely nowhere else, not even for a moment. The place for important papers and documents is in a file folder, appropriately labeled and kept in a designated file drawer. The place for a reminder note to yourself is in the *one* conspicuous place you've decided to keep such notes, and nowhere else.

The same idea applies to more complex things. If you are keeping track of business activities, personal affairs, committee work for a couple of organizations, and numerous other responsibilities, you must be organized. Having separate bins on your desk for each activity, a well-organized file system, a long-range calendar planner, and specific (or enough) time set aside for each responsibility will make handling these multiple tasks and responsibilities possible. Only by being and staying well organized can your brain handle so much going on in your life. When you become absentminded, confused, and mentally worn out, be suspicious that you need to be better organized.

Making It Work for You

What are the things you lose track of most often in your life? List them, then decide why you lose track of them. Is there no consistent place for an item? Are you sloppy about putting something back where it belongs? Do your desk and papers need a little attention to organization? Decide what you can do item by item to eliminate chaos in your basic routines.

40

Visualize—Open Your Mind's Eyes

Visualize whatever you are learning and want to remember. Anytime you listen to, think about, or read something, you can visualize it. Even with something as simple as learning someone's name, visualization dramatizes in your mind what you want to remember. And seeing something, even just in your imagination, makes it more real and vivid. The information becomes mentally active, personalized, and dynamic. Visualization also energizes more brain areas during the act of storing, thus making the material that much easier to retrieve later on.

Let's say you want to remember a new word that has some technical meaning relevant to your work. I learned the name of a primary brain structure involved in memory, the *hippocampus*, by visualizing my alma mater populated with student hippopotami. I've never forgotten the word, and I always smile when I use it. If someone tells you about a movie and you want to see it, visualize what they are telling you so you can recall that visualization and remember to go see the movie. If you read a newspaper story, visualize what's going on. Mentally construct the details. Make the information real to your brain, both in words and in pictures.

The visualization habit is a powerful skill involving much more than mere daydreaming. It is sensory expansion with a purpose. Visualization sets up a mental picture of an event, an idea, a person, or a place. It links the hearing and seeing senses, and interprets information within the individual's unique manner of seeing—in the "mind's eye." The technique of visualization is useful for much more than memory enhancement; it can be a powerful tool for application in many life areas. (For more information, see *Creative Visualization* by Shakti Gawain, Whatever Publishing, Inc., 1978.)

Making It Work for You

Consider the word *olfactory*. If you don't know what it means, look it up in the dictionary. Write down the word to form a visual image of it, making the picture as creative, unusual, even ridiculous, as you can. Create an image that's dynamic, not static and unexciting. Visualize the concept, associate it with other words and ideas that you know, draw or doodle something that you associate with the word, repeat the word often, and use it at the earliest opportunity.

41

Review, Review, Review

Repetition is an excellent way to learn and retain new information. As we're taught in study skills class, "Survey new material, read it, and then review it." Or, as we learn from effective public speakers, "Tell 'em what you're going to tell 'em; tell 'em; then tell 'em what you just told 'em." Re-exposure, review, and repetition all mean the same thing—stronger learning and stronger memory.

Repetition causes your brain to retrace its circuits, so to speak. This makes the memory pattern (and the neural circuits involved) just that much more solid. Many people think that just one reading or hearing of some unfamiliar information should be enough to emblazon it in memory. Although sometimes this is so, most of the time we need to review two, three, or four times before we've "got it." Each review strengthens the memory traces and adds a little bit of new information you might have missed on the first or second reading.

Reviewing information must not be boring. Review should mean a *re-encounter* with the information in some new way: seeing it a little differently, forming new associations and new visualizations, ordering the information a little differently, experiencing an "aha."

Review works best if you have something concrete to start with: notes, an outline, a tape recording, drawings or photographs, underlined material in a book, and so forth. Since reviewing must be active, as any effective learning experience must be, make sure your review is interesting and not drudgery. Reviewing schoolwork with a friend, for example, can be a good way to cinch the learning. Most of all, find creative ways to review: draw pictures or diagrams, make a (more or less) detailed outline, tell or describe the material to someone else.

Making It Work for You

Among the memory tips in this book, several have to do with review in some direct or indirect way. Select the tips that rely on some memory technique that reinforces review of learning to instill it in memory. Notice, to fulfill this little exercise, you'll have to review the 40 tips you've read!

42

Flex Your Mental Muscles

It's fairly easy to get fixed on one idea or solution to a problem. By asking yourself "What is another way of looking at this problem?" you can begin to think of alternatives. It doesn't even matter if the alternatives are right or wrong; just think of them first and evaluate them later. The point is to broaden your mental associations—your mental flexibility. Rigid thinking can spell poor memory because most information is not that concrete or fixed. As with daily life, change must be incorporated into our mental structure.

Encourage yourself to think more deeply or variably about problem solutions. When you remember a particular solution to a problem or situation, ask yourself for another one. This may be difficult at first, but it becomes easier with practice. Forcing yourself to think flexibly will make you more thorough as well as generate more memory associations.

A great mental exercise along these lines is to think of a common object (a brick, a paper clip, a file card, or whatever) and list 20 different uses for it. Or the next time someone asks you why you do something the way you do, stop and consider whether your explanation is the *only* explanation.

What does this have to do with improving your memory? By now you probably realize that flexibility is the key to greater association networks in the brain. The more flexibly you can think, the less you will get stuck trying to think of something and the easier and more spontaneous it will be to form the associations that make recall easier.

Making It Work for You

Challenge yourself to list all the uses for Velcro you can think of. Or pick something you do routinely, the same way all the time (housework, the route you follow driving to work, what you do for recreation). Now, come up with two or three alternatives. The next time you're aware that you are facing a situation in need of problem solving, don't be content with the first solution you come up with. Brainstorm to think of as many solutions as you can. As Carl Sagan observed in *Broca's Brain* (Random House, 1979), "We are an intelligent species and the use of our intelligence quite properly gives us pleasure. In this respect the brain is like a muscle. When it is in use we feel very good. Understanding is joyous."

43

Look Forward and Upward

Never compare yourself with "how you used to be" or with some ideal of how you think you *should* be. Thinking that your memory used to be much better 10 or 20 years ago is self-defeating. Lots of things change how we perceive our memories working. Age, a mild head injury, stress, a chronic illness, poor self-concept, personal insecurity—all can play a role in how your memory functions. Accepting how you are right now, without regrets and without comparison to some ideal (past, present, or future), is crucial to developing a positive and optimistic feeling about yourself and your memory.

We constantly change as we grow older and sometimes interpret that change as bad or as a loss. Just as most people aren't as physically compelling at 40 as at 20, our minds work differently, too. The body doesn't deteriorate over these 20 years, it just changes. So do our physical needs, activities, and interests. In many respects, our minds are richer and fuller at 40 than at 20. A trade-off for richer mental resources can be occasional slower recall.

Whatever your philosophy about the effects of age, brain injury, or illness, don't look back. An acceptance of "now" and a positive outlook about the present and the future is all you need. If you continually compare yourself with how you used to be or how you'd like to be, you may never measure up, leading you into regret, negativity, pessimism, and many failures (since that's what you've come to expect).

So, you ask, if I accept the way I am now, what's the point of reading and practicing these memory tips? Good question. The key concept is that you are okay *now*, just working to make yourself more efficient. Self-acceptance and self-improvement go hand in hand.

Making It Work for You

Think about why optimism is based on a positive acceptance of life right now. Even though the concept of optimism implies a future orientation, it begins with an acceptance of the present. Does this make sense to you?

44

Establish a Routine

Habits are rarely forgotten. While being too much a creature of habit can rob you of spontaneity or creativity, there's value in establishing routines for many of the more mundane and regular things you do. A routine allows you to perform a sequence of tasks without much thinking.

Remembering the many things you must do day to day can be aided by establishing some regular patterns. People with pets, for example, usually find themselves forced into some kind of routine—dogs love 'em. Waking at a regular time, going to the bathroom, playing, eating, and barking at the mail carrier are all expectations that easily become routine for dogs, and the dog's routine often works into the master's as well.

It is essential in forming a routine that each part or component be done each and every time the routine is performed, and in the same sequence (getting up, showering, making coffee, brushing teeth, combing hair, and so forth). This is what a routine is, and the better organized and efficient, the less prone we are to varying it. Spending 45 minutes in a detailed and comprehensive "getting ready" routine assures that you will leave the house without forgetting to put your billfold in your pocket or to turn on your answering machine. Having and performing a morning routine also relieves you of having to make a series of decisions, such as whether or not to take a shower or leave lights on in the house. Want to commit 10 minutes every day to exercise, reading, writing, or listening to motivational tapes? Then make it part of a routine.

Making It Work for You

Decide what you want to accomplish in a short period of time—first thing in the morning, over your lunch break, at the end of the day, or whenever. List every detail you want to accomplish during that time and arrange the items you come up with in the most logical, efficient order. Practice your routine, daily and flawlessly, and you'll be sure to accomplish something you want to do every day.

45

Stack the Deck for Better Retrieval

Information we learn, store, and retrieve must fit into a mental "slot." If it doesn't, it gets lost. Learning—and later remembering—depends on actively compartmentalizing information as you take it in.

Index cards make wonderful learning and memory aids— they allow you to record small amounts of information and then sort and rearrange your stack into categories that make sense to you. Perhaps you might color-code cards to represent different kinds of information. Index cards can help you learn and remember factual information, names of people, anniversaries and birthdays, inventories, business contacts, instructions, book lists, and so forth.

Using index cards is simply one more way to get yourself mentally organized. It may require some ingenuity and creativity to categorize information onto colored cards, but doing so makes learning and recall considerably easier. Your categories might be word definitions, regional jokes, types of recipes, steps in a sequence, names and addresses of business contacts, memory enhancement techniques, and so forth. If you're a professional who needs to keep track of a large variety of products and/or services, compile a set of cards that contain descriptions, uses, costs, and availability. Then, by categorizing the cards in different ways, you can learn your business easily. (If you want to get even fancier, there are software programs for personal computers that let you do this same thing electronically, calling up any combinations of information you want. The key is to organize the information in the first place.)

Just remember that *any* information makes more sense and is more easily learned and recalled if you can fit it into a compartment or category.

Making It Work for You

Using a source of information such as a newspaper article, a chapter in a textbook, or a lecture, identify and write down categories that you can recognize in the piece. Start with an overall key concept, then branch out as necessary. The categories you come up with may or may not be peg words from the main body of the information; they need to function as a label for a class or type or subgroup of the information. A newspaper editorial, for example, might have two broad categories to start with: fact and opinion. From there you can identify subcategories. Practice with this type of categorical thinking greatly helps in becoming a more organized thinker.

46

A Quiet Mind Promotes Learning

Avoid distractions when you are actively learning new information. The television, a nearby conversation, a physical pain, a disturbing emotional state, some "unfinished business" on your mind, kids vying for your attention—all these things will inhibit new learning and, hence, recall.

When you really need to learn something, give it your complete and undivided attention. Find a place and time where and when you won't be distracted. Commit yourself to doing so, avoiding such pitfalls as "I just can't find the time" or "There's no place I can go without being interrupted." Both of these statements reflect hidden priorities that sabotage the intended new learning. If you really want to find the time and place, you will! Remember, you can't recall something you haven't learned well in the first place.

Often we approach learning half-heartedly and then complain that we can't learn or remember what we're supposed to. Learning requires full commitment. If you can't commit, find out why, then take corrective control. If you're not really committed to learning in the first place, you're not being honest with yourself when you blame your failure to learn on a poor memory.

Making It Work for You

You may see a contradiction to this memory tip: Some people find that they can concentrate *much better* on something if they *do* have the television or the stereo blasting. Can you explain why? Decide for yourself if a quiet or a noisy environment is best for your concentration.

47

Question Everything

Questioning arouses curiosity and interest. A great way to remember, therefore, is to ask yourself a question about the fact or idea you want to learn or recall. By generating questions about information or situations, your mind starts to link associations. Thinking becomes dynamic and exciting. Questioning incites a dialogue within yourself that frees up the mind and stimulates its natural links.

Questioning works both for learning and for remembering. When you are learning something for the first time, questions you generate about the material will enhance your involvement and make the learning interesting—the learning is answering your personal questions. When you are trying to recall something but can't remember it right away, start asking questions of yourself to get unblocked. You'll begin answering other questions instead of becoming upset over what you can't remember.

For example, if you are trying to recall the name of someone you see pictured in your mind, start asking yourself questions about the person: Where did you last see her? What was she wearing? What were you talking about? Instead of staying stuck on one aspect—the person's name—you're now broadening your recall by asking mind-jarring questions. This stimulates the associative pathways in your brain.

Making It Work for You

To see how you can enhance learning through the use of questioning, select a magazine article that just by title alone you think might interest you. Before you read the article, ask yourself exactly what questions you want the article to answer. Now read the article. Whenever you wonder whether the article is going to answer your question, think of some other questions the article is leading up to answering. This technique keeps your attention up, makes the information personally interesting, and enables your brain to store and retrieve the information more easily.

The difference between active and passive learning—and remembering—is the extent to which you are personally involved. Asking questions, out loud and directly or just silently to yourself, primes your brain to receive the information that will answer them.

48

Observe the Forest AND the Trees

Observe the parts in order to remember the wholes. Your mind's natural tendency is to pay attention first to the general, the overall, the "big picture." So, to remember something such as a car, a person, a place, or an idea that is not particularly unusual in general, force yourself to go beyond the mind's natural limits and find things specifically unique about this thing or person or idea.

Too often we see things but don't really intensify our vision and make it *observing*. Although observing is a skill you can easily learn, it takes a little conscious effort. We need to learn to see with the conscious intention to observe. Even something as simple as taking note of the color of someone's eyes, hair, or complexion when being introduced will help you remember his or her name and the context in which you met. This occurs because by focusing this way you are personalizing the memory and making the whole impression more detailed and more vivid. You are adding bits to your memory that can all fit together. The more pieces your brain has to draw on to identify the whole, the easier you can recall things later on.

Details help to create mental pegs on which memories are hung. The details must be unusual or special in some way as well as meaningful. Trivial or unrelated details that lack uniqueness won't provide any special reason for remembering them.

Making It Work for You

The next time you meet someone, consciously observe his or her eye color, hair color, cheek bones, lip shape, neck, clothing—any and all details that you can bring into your consciousness. Not only will that person quickly stand out as unique, but you will remember him or her because of what you have observed. Further, writing down your observations in a journal or diary helps you retain them even more.

49

Find Your Place and Time for Learning and Remembering

Set aside a special place and time for learning. Especially if you are learning new and formal information (such as in a course or a new job procedure), having a specific place and time to learn establishes the "mental set" for learning and minimizes distractions. A desk or table that you use consistently for learning will put you in the mood to learn when you sit there, as opposed to plopping down in your easy chair, lying in bed, or using the kitchen table. Also, once you've selected your place for learning or performing a specific task, try not to carry out other tasks there.

This concept emphasizes the psychological idea of "set." A specific task performed at a specific place will feel more natural and will take place more efficiently because the mind has been "set" to function in a specific way—learning.

Sometimes people can cultivate a real boost to their learning, creativity, and memory by strongly associating a place to study with actually being creative. The more your mind is set to learn (or create), the more effective your memory will be for learning and creating. If you can cut out distractions and surround yourself with things that are conducive to learning and remembering (the right papers, pens, typewriter, computer, books, and so forth), the more you will become fully engaged in and enjoy learning—and remembering.

Making It Work for You

Think of a special place that might take on a "set" for you to learn or do something creative. If you want to write poetry, for example, is there a specific place where you feel "poetic" and think would be conductive to performing this task well?

50

Minimize Competition to Maximize Self-Confidence

Competition often causes us to focus on our shortcomings instead of our strengths. When intimidated by the potential of someone overtaking us, it is easy to give in. After all, there is only one winner and all the rest are losers. Competition creates many losers.

How does this relate to memory? Self-confidence is the number-one memory builder. Without self-confidence and a realistic belief in yourself, you will have a difficult time learning, remembering, or doing anything. If you constantly compare yourself with others and see yourself in a disadvantaged position, you will soon learn to perceive yourself as a failure because you will believe you cannot compete.

Competition often defeats positive thinking about yourself. It has the tendency to erode self-confidence and makes us compare ourselves with others, often unrealistically. So, give up thinking competitively and just do the best you can at anything. You will know what your best is; you don't have to compare yourself with anyone else to determine that.

Making It Work for You

What are some areas (activities) of your life where you see yourself in competition? How can you minimize that competition and lift yourself above it?

The Author

Dennis P. Swiercinsky, Ph.D., is a psychologist who has specialized in neuropsychological diagnosis and treatment for the past 20 years. He has worked with hundreds of persons and has taught numerous workshops on how to improve brain function, including learning and memory. He has written four books on specialized psychological assessment and has numerous scientific articles to his credit. He has also published magazine and newspaper articles on topics related to brain functioning, learning, and memory. Dr. Swiercinsky continues to teach and write in such areas as creativity, personal values, and intellectual and mind expansion.

This book reflects the accumulation of techniques Dr. Swiercinsky has used with a wide variety of persons who seek self-improvement. He continues to develop programs in memory and intellectual improvement in the course of his clinical practice in the greater Kansas City area.